W9-AAY-697

Living with ADHD
A Practical Guide to Coping with Attention Deficit Hyperactivity Disorder

*For parents, teachers, physicians
and all those who care for children with ADHD*

By Rebecca Kajander, CPNP, MPH

in conjunction with

Institute for Research and Education
HealthSystem Minnesota
Minneapolis, Minnesota

This book is dedicated to the memory of Jeffrey L. Alexander, M.D. Dr. Alexander was a loved and gifted pediatrician who specialized in caring for children with developmental disabilities, including ADHD. He believed that every child and family could turn the negative to positive, if given appropriate skills and support in their life journey.

Foreword

A tribute to
Jeffrey L. Alexander
1944–1993

During his career, he helped many children rise above difficulties. He could see beyond a child's negative behavior— past the wild activity, the angry or sad face, or the failing school grades. He sought out each child's unique strengths and convinced both child and family to refocus their energy positively. Stories of lives he helped change are numerous. With humor and enthusiasm he conveyed his unshakable belief in the often hidden talents of his patients, and most importantly, made them believe in themselves.

The same ability to recognize the talents of others allowed him to assemble and manage a multidisciplinary team, which he did with the founding of the Alexander Center for Child Development and Behavior in 1980. Part of the Park Nicollet Clinic HealthSystem Minnesota, the Alexander Center carries on Dr. Alexander's vision and draws upon the skills of professionals from many disciplines to address the needs of children with developmental, behavioral, educational, or emotional concerns. These disciplines include pediatrics, psychology, education, speech and language, and nursing. In line with Dr. Alexander's philosophy, the Center works closely with the pediatric community, schools, and community resources to ensure that clients and their families receive the care and support they need and deserve.

Dr. Alexander is remembered and admired for his vision, his boundless energy and his dedication to children. He was a caring doctor and a willing mentor. He is dearly missed.

"There is something that is much more scarce, something finer by far, something rarer than ability. It is the ability to recognize ABILITY."

—Elbert Hubbard

Table of Contents

If you are the parent of a child who has attention deficit hyperactivity disorder (ADHD), you know the daily challenges and joys of living with the neurodevelopmental disorder of ADHD. You may even have ADHD yourself. There's no doubt about it—living with ADHD isn't always easy. Yet, there are many things that you and your child can do to manage the symptoms of ADHD. That's what this book is all about.

This guide isn't a scientific discussion of ADHD. Many excellent resources already provide that (see Chapter 7 for a list). Instead, this guide provides some practical, tried-and-true tips that can help you and your child cope better with everyday events—at home, at school, and in social settings. These tips were gathered from health care providers, therapists, teachers, and parents of children with ADHD. Not every idea will work for every child at every age. You are encouraged to try them and find the ones that work best with your child's special personality.

Following are a few key points about ADHD to keep in mind:

- ADHD is *not* a disease; it's the way the brain works. ADHD can't be cured, but it can be *managed.*
- Your child was *born* with ADHD. It is a lifelong condition.
- Managing ADHD is a *team* effort: It requires the dedicated efforts of a group of professionals working together, including health care providers, behavioral therapists, teachers, school personnel—and you and your child.
- Your child's ADHD was *not* caused by your parenting style.

You are not alone!

One More Thing...

ADHD is an inherited condition—one or both parents of a child with ADHD may also have ADHD. If you recognize any of the symptoms of ADHD in your family tree, or if you had similar experiences as a child (for example, trouble concentrating in school or being called "daydreamer," "hard to handle," "hyper," or "wild"), it's possible that *you* have ADHD. Because most people don't outgrow ADHD, adults with this condition may have trouble organizing tasks, concentrating for long periods, or remembering instructions.

Some adults can benefit from ADHD medication. There are also many techniques that adults can learn to help them improve their organization, memory, and communication skills. If you suspect that you have ADHD, you may want to talk with your health care provider about being evaluated. In addition, Chapter 7 of this guide lists organizations and resources that can help you learn more about ADHD.

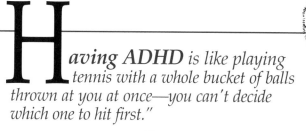

"**H**aving ADHD** is like playing tennis with a whole bucket of balls thrown at you at once—you can't decide which one to hit first."

—Tony, age 17

Parents may be tempted to blame a child who has ADHD for being deliberately willful or overactive—especially when everyone's nerves are frayed by the latest outburst at school or another trip to the store cut short by a temper tantrum. For

Chapter 1

Understanding ADHD

parents, simply knowing that their child often *can't*—not won't—control disruptive behaviors may be the first step in learning to manage ADHD. In fact, the more that you, your child, and the people important in your child's life learn about ADHD, the easier it will be to live with this challenging condition.

What Is ADHD?

ADHD is a neurodevelopmental disorder. *Neuro* means affecting the brain; *developmental* means that symptoms change as the person grows older. ADHD is a hereditary condition that affects about 1 in 25 children in the United States. It is five times more common in boys than in girls.

Having ADHD is something like listening to a radio with poor reception. Instead of being able to tune in one station clearly, you end up hearing many channels at once. This type of "static" makes it difficult to tune in or concentrate on any one thing for very long.

ADHD is *not a disease*. It's the way a person's brain works. In a person who has ADHD, the parts of the brain that control the ability to maintain attention and stop inappropriate behavior are not as well developed as they could be. Studies show that people with ADHD may have less blood flow and chemical activity in these parts of the brain. This may explain why children who have ADHD often are inattentive, impulsive, and hyperactive.

•**Inattentive.** The inattentive child has trouble focusing attention and tuning out irrelevant sights, sounds, and even thoughts. He or she is easily distracted by movement, noises, smells, or colors, and may spend a lot of time daydreaming. Being distracted can cause the child to lose focus and miss the main point or the big picture. This child often appears not to be listening, and has trouble finishing one task before beginning another. The inattentive child may also have trouble putting together and using several pieces of information.

•**Impulsive.** The impulsive child shifts frequently from one activity to another, has trouble waiting his or her turn, and often speaks or acts before thinking about consequences (such as running into the street without looking for cars). This child interrupts often, monopolizes conversations, is easily frustrated or angered, and tends to be bossy when playing with other children.

•**Hyperactive.** The hyperactive child seems to move constantly. He or she has trouble channeling actions into productive outcomes, finds it hard to sit still, and may talk nonstop. Hyperactive children are often described as "bouncing off the walls, wiggly, squirmy, tireless, chatterboxes, and always into everything."

The Difference Between ADD and ADHD

The difference between ADD and ADHD can be confusing. Not all children with attention problems are hyperactive, but they may have a lot of trouble paying attention.

Over the years, the words used to describe attentional problems have changed often and will change again. Some researchers believe that ADD and ADHD may be two different disorders, but others believe they are the same disorder with overlapping symptoms. The current diagnostic terms call everything ADHD and then describe three different types of ADHD:

ADHD—primarily attentive type
ADHD—primarily hyperactive/impulsive type
ADHD—combined type

Here are some differences between ADHD-Inattentive Type and ADHD-Hyperactive Type. (For more information, see also page 7, Criteria for Diagnosing Attention Deficit/Hyperactivity Disorder.)

Inattentive Type	Hyperactive/Impulsive Type
Hypoactive or lethargic	Motoric hyperactive
Daydreaming or "spacey"	Short attention span
Trouble focusing on the right information	Trouble stopping oneself from responding to all stimuli
Forgetful	Impulsive
Few behavior problems	More behavior problems
More common in girls	More common in boys
Not seen in preschool children	Seen in children as young as three years old

Note: For ease in reading, both conditions are called ADHD in this guide. Most of the tips and suggestions apply to both ADD and ADHD.

How Is ADHD Diagnosed?

Diagnosing ADHD can be difficult for several reasons. Symptoms of ADHD are unpredictable and variable—they may not be apparent in all situations, they change with age, and they vary from child to child. There is no blood test or brain wave test to diagnose ADHD. Certain medical diseases, behavioral or emotional conditions, and learning disabilities can show symptoms similar to ADHD. These other conditions must be considered before ADHD can be accurately diagnosed. They can also occur together. For example, some children may have both ADHD and learning disabilities.

ADHD is diagnosed by carefully evaluating a child's medical, developmental, behavioral, social/emotional, and academic histories. In addition, complete physical and neurological exams are recommended to rule out any physiological or nervous system problems. For most children with ADHD, these exams are essentially normal. Assessing the child's developmental, behavioral, social/emotional, and academic status shows how the child is progressing in relation to his or her age group.

There are also a number of tools to help doctors, therapists, and teachers decide whether a child has ADHD. One standard tool is the *Diagnostic and Statistical Manual of Mental Disorders (DSM-IV)*; published in 1994, it lists behaviors that may indicate ADD and ADHD. These criteria, shown below, help professionals diagnose whether a child may have one or more of these conditions.

Criteria for Diagnosing Attention Deficit Hyperactivity Disorder

A.The child must satisfy the criteria for either (1) or (2) as follows:

(1) Six (or more) of the following symptoms of inattention that have lasted for at least six months, to a degree that is maladaptive and inappropriate for the child's age:

a) Often fails to give close attention to details or makes careless mistakes in schoolwork, work, or other activities

b) Often has difficulty maintaining attention in tasks or play activities

c) Often does not seem to listen when spoken to directly

d) Often does not follow through on instructions and fails to finish schoolwork, chores, or duties in the workplace (not due to oppositional behavior or failure to understand directions)

e) Often has difficulty organizing tasks and activities

f) Often avoids, dislikes, or is reluctant to engage in tasks that require sustained mental effort (such as schoolwork or homework)

g) Often loses things necessary for tasks or activities (for example, toys, school assignments, pencils, books, or tools)

h) Often is easily distracted by extraneous stimuli

i) Often is forgetful in daily activities

(2) Six (or more) of the following symptoms of hyperactivity-impulsivity that have lasted for at least six months to a degree that is maladaptive and inappropriate for the child's age:

Hyperactivity

a) Often fidgets with hands or feet, or squirms in seat

b) Often leaves seat in classroom, or in other situations in which remaining seated is expected

c) Often runs about or climbs excessively in situations in which it is inappropriate (in adolescents or adults, may be related to feelings of restlessness)

d) Often has difficulty playing or engaging in leisure activities quietly

e) Often is "on the go" or acts as if "driven by a motor"

f) Often talks excessively

Impulsivity

g) Often blurts out answers before questions have been completed

h) Often has difficulty awaiting turn

i) Often interrupts or intrudes on others (for example, interrupts conversations or butts into games)

B. Some hyperactive-impulsive or inattentive symptoms were present before the age of 7 years.

C. Some impairment from the symptoms is present in two or more settings (for example, in school and at home).

D. There must be clear evidence of clinically significant impairment in social, academic, or occupational functioning.

E. The symptoms do not occur exclusively during the course of a pervasive developmental disorder, schizophrenia, or other psychotic disorder, and are not better accounted for by another mental disorder (for example, mood disorder, anxiety disorder, dissociative disorder, or a personality disorder).

A child can have many of these behaviors and not have ADD or ADHD. The criteria should serve as a red flag for parents and teachers who are concerned about a child's behavior at home and at school. If a child shows many of the behaviors listed above, parents should consider having him or her tested by a team of qualified professionals.

After the child is tested, a diagnosis can be made in one of these three categories:

I. Attention Deficit/Hyperactivity Disorder—Combined Type. This diagnosis is made when a child has six (or more) symptoms from both Category A(1) (inattention) and Category A(2) (hyperactivity/impulsivity).

II. Attention Deficit/Hyperactivity Disorder—Predominately Inattentive Type. This diagnosis is made if a child has six or more symptoms from Category A(1) (inattention) but *not* Category A(2) (hyperactivity/impulsivity).

III. Attention Deficit/Hyperactivity Disorder—Predominately Hyperactive/Impulsive Type. This diagnosis is made if a child has six or more symptoms from Category A(2) (hyperactivity/impulsivity) but *not* Category A(1) (inattention).

Understanding Disruptive Behavior Disorders

A disruptive behavior disorder is defined as a pattern of behavior that is disruptive in social situations and negatively affects the rights of other people. ADHD is one kind of disruptive behavior disorder. Other types of specific disruptive behavior disorders include oppositional defiant disorder (ODD) and conduct disorder (CD).

It is important to understand ODD and CD because many children with ADHD will also have ODD and CD. Children with ODD and CD will also have significantly more problems as adolescents and adults than children who have only ADHD.

Criteria for Diagnosing Oppositional Defiant Disorder (ODD)

A. The child has five (or more) of the following symptoms that have lasted for at least six months:

(1) Often loses temper

(2) Often argues with adults

(3) Often actively defies or refuses adult requests or rules

(4) Often deliberately does things that annoy other people

(5) Often blames others for his or her own mistakes

(6) Is often touchy or easily annoyed by others

(7) Is often angry or resentful

(8) Is often spiteful or vindictive

(9) Often swears or uses obscene language

B. The child does not meet criteria for conduct disorder, and symptoms do not occur exclusively during the course of a psychotic disorder, dysthymia or a major depressive, hypomanic or manic episode.

Criteria for Diagnosing Conduct Disorder (CD)

The child must have three (or more) of the following symptoms that have lasted at least six months:

(1) Has stolen without confrontation of a victim on more than one occasion (including forgery)

(2) Has run away from home overnight at least twice (or once without returning) while living in parental or parental surrogate home

(3) Often lies (other than to avoid physical or sexual abuse)

(4) Has deliberately engaged in fire setting

(5) Is often truant from school (or work, if adolescent)

(6) Has broken into someone else's house, building or car

(7) Has deliberately destroyed others' property (other than by setting fires)

(8) Has been physically cruel to animals

(9) Has forced someone into sexual activity with him or her

(10) Has used a weapon in more than one fight

(11) Often initiates physical fights

(12) Has stolen with confrontation of a victim

(13) Has been physically cruel to people

"*ADHD is not a disorder of knowing what to do, but of doing what one knows.*"

—Russell Barkley, PhD

ADHD and the Nature of Self-Control

Russell Barkley, PhD, is one of the nation's leading researchers on ADHD. He and others have suggested that ADHD may not be *only* about paying attention. Barkley states that ADHD is "a deficiency of self-control"—having difficulty being in control of where (and on what) you choose to focus your attention. With ADHD, then, the problem is not taking in information or paying attention to information; it is controlling one's response to the information. Tuning out distractions, attending to the most important information, and keeping one's attention long enough all are needed. Some children may also have trouble stopping themselves from responding to everything in their environment. They may have difficulty continuing a task for an appropriate length of time or pausing between tasks. Some children can pay attention to video games and other activities they enjoy for long periods of time. They may even get so "hyperfocused" on something that it is hard to get their attention. These difficulties occur because of the weak development in the parts of the brain that control attention, organization, planning and problem solving. In other words, they may have trouble controlling attention.

Barkley has defined four "executive functions" in the brain that are needed for self control of attention:

(1) Active working memory. This is the ability to keep information in your memory while you are doing something else. It involves having a good awareness of time and being able to think about the past and future. For example, a child is given three instructions. After starting the first instruction, he or she may forget the second and third.

(2) Internalization of speech. Internal language is needed to plan and organize actions. After the age of five, most children stop talking out loud about their thinking. Some children, on the other hand, continue to talk excessively because they "think out loud" all the time.

(3) Self-regulation of affect. Self-regulation of affect is the ability to control emotions, to set aside negative emotions—disappointment and frustration, for instance—and use positive emotions to plan and organize thoughts and decisions.

(4) Reconstitution. Reconstitution is the ability to select and choose a plan of action.

Here is an example of using executive functions:

Sarah needs to stop working on the computer to eat dinner and go to dance lessons. She needs to remember to save her work and exit from her program while she tells her mom that she will come and eat dinner (active memory). She must think through the steps of saving her work (internal speech), deal with her frustration at not wanting to stop (affect control) and decide when she will be able to get back to her work (reconstitution).

Five Key Strategies for Managing ADHD

A lot has been written in recent years about using medication to manage ADHD. In most cases, medication helps children with ADHD to calm down and focus their attention on the task at hand. But medication alone is rarely the most effective way to manage ADHD. To achieve the best results medication, if needed, should be combined with other approaches.

There are five key elements to successful ADHD management:

1. Academic modifications: Adjusting the school setting, which can range from classroom seating to special education services.

2. Parent education: Educating parents about ADHD—what they can do to help their child cope, and how they can advocate for their child.

3. Child understanding: Helping the child understand the cause of the condition, strategies for managing it, and the proper use of medications.

4. Individual/family counseling: Working with a counselor to develop ways to change individual behaviors or family dynamics to provide better structure and support for the child.

5. Medication: Working with a health care provider to determine whether medications will be helpful and, if so, the proper dosage and frequency.

These strategies are described in more detail later in this guide.

*"**T**he pills didn't make me do my schoolwork, but when I decided to do it, the pills helped me concentrate."*

—Marcus, age 11

Chapter 2

Getting the Most from Medications

Some people with ADHD say that using medication is similar to wearing glasses: It brings everything into sharper focus. Others say that it's like putting the brain into "cruise control"—it helps your brain get to the right speed, and then helps it stay there.

Many parents are concerned about using medication to control their child's ADHD symptoms. Although the medication is safe, parents often worry that their child will become addicted to it or suffer harmful side effects. Children are often concerned, too. They worry about taking "drugs," or about what the other kids will think when they go to the school nurse for their dose of medication.

Research shows that medication can help the majority of children who have ADHD. However, medication should not be used as the only way to treat ADHD. Instead it should serve as a "gateway" that supports behavioral and educational techniques.

ADHD medications affect people in different ways. One type of medication might work well for some, while another might work better for others. The kind and amount of medication may fluctuate, depending on age, body size, and choice of activity. For example, medication may help a child concentrate on homework or pay attention during sports.

Unlike some other medications designed for long-term use, ADHD medication must be monitored regularly. Every child's treatment plan is different, because the medication's effectiveness varies from one child to another. It's important that parents take an active role in working with their child's health care provider to design a medication program appropriate for their child.

Several types of medications are used to treat ADHD. Methylphenidate (Ritalin®) and dextroamphetamine (Dexedrine®) are used most often, but other medications may also be prescribed. The chart at the end of this chapter lists medications commonly used to treat ADHD.

Ritalin: Questions and Answers

Ritalin, the brand name of methylphenidate, is the most widely used medication for treating ADHD. You may have questions about how Ritalin works and whether it is safe. The next few pages should answer many of your questions. If you have other questions about Ritalin—or any other medication—be sure to ask your child's health care provider.

What is Ritalin?

Ritalin is a stimulant medication used to control the symptoms of ADHD—short attention span, impulsive behavior, and hyperactivity. The fact that Ritalin is a stimulant often confuses parents. If correctly prescribed, Ritalin will not make your child more hyperactive.

What does Ritalin do?

Ritalin acts on the parts of the brain responsible for sustaining attention. It increases alertness, allowing a child to concentrate for longer periods of time. With improved concentration, the child is better able to organize thoughts and plan actions.

How is Ritalin taken?

Ritalin is taken in tablet form. The tablet is small, easy to swallow, and may be taken with meals. It begins to work about 30 minutes after it is swallowed, reaches peak benefit in 1 to 2 hours, and leaves the body in 3 to 5 hours. Most children who have ADHD take Ritalin two or three times a day.

Dosage varies from one child to the next, due to differences in the child's nervous system and in the way the body absorbs the medicine. The correct dose is usually determined during a trial period—perhaps six weeks. Parents and teachers need to work closely with the health care provider during the trial period to carefully observe and record the child's behavior.

What are the benefits of Ritalin?

The most common benefits include:

- Calming effect—the child is less active, less excitable, and less impulsive
- Increased ability to deal with frustration
- More time spent doing quiet eye-hand tasks
- Better completion of tasks and assignments
- Greater ability to follow directions
- Fewer mood swings
- Improved behavior in group and social activities

Is Ritalin safe?

Ritalin has been used and studied since the 1940s. It has proven to be a very safe medication. Most side effects are temporary and/or easily managed.

What are the side effects of Ritalin?

The most common side effects are loss of appetite, trouble falling asleep, mild headaches, stomach aches, and irritability.

If they occur, side effects usually subside within two to four weeks. If your child continues to experience side effects, talk with your doctor, who may be able to adjust the dosage or prescribe a different medication.

If your child develops physical tics (such as eye blinking, shrugging, sniffing or throat clearing), skin rash, or severe irritability, stop the medication and call your doctor immediately.

What are the signs of too much Ritalin?

Overdoses of Ritalin are very rare. A child who is very withdrawn, tearful, whiny, or overly anxious may have taken too much Ritalin. The symptoms of an overdose include vomiting, agitation, tremors, convulsions, and/or hallucinations. If your child has any symptoms that concern you, stop the medication and call your doctor.

How do children feel about taking Ritalin?

Children whose performance in school improves while they take Ritalin often experience a boost in self-esteem. Their relationships with peers and adults are also likely to be more positive. These children generally have a positive or neutral attitude about taking Ritalin. A child's attitude will also be affected by parents', teachers', or peers' attitude about taking Ritalin—or any other medication.

Does Ritalin have any effect on learning?

Stimulant medication often increases the amount and quality of schoolwork completed. Thoughts or information may be processed at a faster rate. The child may have improved handwriting and better short-term memory. However, medication does not make a child smarter, nor can it be used to treat a learning disability.

How long are children usually treated with Ritalin?

The length of treatment varies. Most children will need to take medication for several years. As a general rule, one-third of children benefit from medication until puberty, one-third take medication through college, and one-third use medication as adults. This is because the severity of ADHD can vary, and some people outgrow the symptoms.

To determine whether medication is still needed each school year, a one– to two– week period without medication should be tried during the school year, in conjunction with your health care provider. The child's school performance and behavior can be closely monitored during this time to see if he or she should continue the medication.

Tips for Using ADHD Medication

The following tips are intended for parents who give medication to younger children, and for teens who take medication without parental supervision.

- **Always consult your doctor before making any change in frequency or dosage of medication.**

- Talk with the school nurse about the best way to give the medication, if your child needs a midday dose. (Children are not allowed to take their own medication at school.) Young children may need the teacher's or nurse's help to remember to take their medication.

- Keep a record of how your child reacts to the medication. Write down any side effects or behavior changes so you can discuss them with your doctor.

- Talk with your child about the advantages of taking medication prior to tutoring, homework, and sports.

- Emphasize to your child that the medication helps him or her concentrate, but it is not a "be smart" or a "be good" pill. Instead, it helps your child slow down and think about making good choices.

- Help your child identify what he or she can do more easily when taking medication.

- Develop a system for taking the medication that's easy to remember. For example, if the medication can be taken with food, always give it at the beginning of the meal. Try posting a weekly calendar on the refrigerator or the bathroom mirror. Let young children put a sticker on the calendar each time they take a dose. For older kids, try using a magnetic board with colored dots or a pill box divided into seven compartments or "days."

If your child is currently taking an ADHD medication...

What did you expect from this medication?

_____

_____

What did your child expect?

_____

_____

What has improved with the use of medication?

_____

_____

What problems still exist?

_____

_____

_____

• Consider using a generic version of the ADHD medication, if available. Generic drugs usually work just as well, and are less expensive. If you switch to a generic version, monitor its effectiveness for a while. If you and your child are disappointed by the results, or if your child is feeling side effects that have lasted longer than a few weeks, check with your doctor. It may be possible to change medications or adjust the frequency and dosage to improve your child's ability to function.

Especially for Teens: Using Medications

• You can take an active part in making decisions about your medication. For example, you may need to attend classes or play a sport both with and without your medication, to see how your performance varies.

• Studies show that long-term use of prescribed medications does not increase your risk for drug abuse.

• Teens who have ADHD are more likely to experience anxiety and depression—which may require different medication. In addition you may want to find someone to talk to about your feelings.

• The daily amount of stimulant medication needed by teenagers relative to body weight is often less than that needed by younger children. Because you weigh more doesn't mean you'll need a higher dose of medication.

• Experts believe that 50 to 70 percent of children with ADHD continue to have problems with short attention spans and impulsive behavior into adolescence and adulthood. Learn as many coping skills as you can to help you function now and in the future.

• The main reason many teens stop taking medication is because they don't want to be "different" than their friends. However, taking your medication may help you act more like your friends.

• Your medicine is prescribed only for you. Never share it with anyone else.

Commonly Used ADHD Medications

This chart lists the medications used most often to treat ADHD. This information is provided so that you can discuss possible options with your health care provider.

Brand Name	Generic Name	What Are the Advantages?	How Is It Usually Taken?
Ritalin®	Methylphenidate	Works quickly (within 30 to 60 minutes); effective in 70% of patients; good safety record	Tablet; 2 - 3 times daily
Ritalin-SR®	Methylphenidate	Especially useful for teens to avoid noontime dose; good safety record	Tablet; 1 - 2 times daily
Dexedrine®	Dextroamphetamine	Works quickly (within 30 to 60 minutes); may avoid noontime dose in capsule form; good safety record	Tablet, capsule, or liquid; 2 - 3 times daily
Dexedrine Spansule®	(No generic)	Lasts about 8 hours; eliminates noontime dose	One capsule daily
Cylert®	Pemoline	Chewable tablet	One tablet daily
Tofranil®	Imipramine hydrochloride	Helpful for children/teens who also have depression or anxiety; lasts throughout the day	Tablet; 1 - 2 times daily
Nopramin®	Desipramine hydrochloride	Helpful for children/teens who also have depression or anxiety; lasts throughout the day	Tablet; 1 - 2 times daily
Catapres®	Clonidine hydrochloride	Helpful for children/teens who also have tic disorder or severe hyperactivity and/or aggression	Tablet; 2 - 4 times daily, or patch worn on skin; changed 1 - 2 times/week
Adderall®	Combination of amphetamine and dextroamphetamine	May eliminate noon dose; can divide for small doses; approved for young children	Tablet; 1 - 2 times daily
Wellbutrin®	Bupropion hydrochloride	Helpful for children with ADHD and depression	Tablet; 1 - 3 times daily
Tenex®	Guanfacine	Helpful for children/teens who also have tic disorder or severe hyperactivity and/or aggression	Tablet; 1 - 2 times

How Long Does It Usually Last?	What Are the Possible Side Effects?	What Are the Cautions?
3 to 4 hours	Difficulty sleeping, decreased appetite, weight loss, headache, irritability, stomach ache	Not recommended for patients with marked anxiety, motor tics, or family history of Tourette Syndrome
About 7 hours	Difficulty sleeping, decreased appetite, weight loss, headache, irritability, stomach ache	Slow onset of action (1 to 2 hours) not recommended for patients with marked anxiety, motor tics, or family history of Tourette Syndrome
3 to 4 hours (tablet)	Difficulty sleeping, decreased appetite, weight loss, headache, irritability, stomach ache	Not recommended for patients with marked anxiety, motor tics, or family history of Tourette Syndrome
8 to 10 hours (Spansule)	Same as above	Same as above
12 to 24 hours	Difficulty sleeping, agitation, headache, stomach ache; abnormal liver function tests (rare)	May take 2 to 4 weeks for clinical response; regular blood tests needed to check liver function
12 to 24 hours	Dry mouth, decreased appetite, headache, stomach ache, dizziness, constipation; rapid heartbeat	May take 2 to 8 weeks for clinical response; baseline ECG may be ordered, and blood work is necessary *Should be discontinued gradually*
12 to 24 hours	Dry mouth, decreased appetite, headache, stomach ache, dizziness, constipation, mild rapid heartbeat	May take 2 to 8 weeks for clinical response; baseline ECG may be ordered, and blood work is necessary *Should be discontinued gradually*
3 to 6 hours (tablet); 5 - 7 days (patch)	Drowsiness, low blood, pressure, headache, dizziness, stomach ache, nausea, dry mouth; localized skin reactions with patch	Stopping medication suddenly could cause an increase in blood pressure; starting dose should be given at bedtime and increased slowly to avoid daytime tiredness
5 to 6 hours	Loss of appetite and weight loss, insomnia, tics, dizziness irritability (most common)	Not recommended for patients with high anxiety, tics or Tourette Syndrome
7 to 15 hours	Difficulty sleeping, decreased appetite, weight loss irritability, stomach ache	Not recommended for patients with tics
6 to 12 hours	Difficulty sleeping, dry mouth, rash, tics, headache. constipation	Not recommended for patients with high blood pressure

Ten-year-old Maria often forgot her homework in the rush to catch the school bus. It was still on her desk or the dining room table—but hardly ever with Maria. Forgetting her homework was affecting Maria's grades. One night, Maria's dad put a basket on a table near the front door. He asked her to put everything in the basket that she needed for school the next day—

homework, gym clothes, and art supplies. Now Maria checks the basket every morning on her way out the door. She's only forgotten her homework once!

This example shows how one simple thing—putting a "school basket" by the front door—made a big difference in Maria's life. There are a lot of other things—some simple, some not so simple—that you can do to make home life easier for your child with ADHD, and for other members of the family.

This chapter offers general parenting guidelines for parents of children with ADHD. It also provides practical tips for managing daily routines, building better behavior, helping siblings cope and, finally, survival tips for parents. The chapter also includes a list of ways to help teens deal more effectively with family rules and expectations.

General Parenting Guidelines

• Try to prevent problems, rather than correct them. There are often simple ways to help your child "do it right" the first time. Many of the suggestions in this chapter are geared to help you do that.

• Be clear with directions. Because your child may have trouble remembering directions, it's important to clearly explain what you want, and ask your child to repeat the directions. More time will be spent on directions, later in this chapter.

• Be firm and consistent with rules and routines. Explain what you want in simple words or phrases, and refuse to argue. Stick with it, even if, at times, bending the rules might be easier. Consistency pays off in the end.

• Praise your child often, to help build his or her self-esteem. Look for things your child does well, then give praise sincerely. Most children are good at spotting false praise, and may not believe you the next time.

• Go easy on criticism and nagging. Constant criticism damages self-esteem. And nagging rarely works, since most children learn early to tune it out. The next time you're tempted to criticize or nag, pause for 10 seconds and try to find a more positive way to say what you're feeling.

• Talk about it. Each time your child makes a poor choice, talk about what happened and about other ways to handle the situation. Help your child see that he or she can make better choices next time.

• Enjoy your child. Children with ADHD can be fun and very creative. By learning to focus on—and enjoy—the positive aspects of your child's personality, some of the difficult behaviors may seem less overwhelming.

As one parent observed, "It's a lot of work parenting Karl. Sometimes I lose my cool and make mistakes. But when I'm patient and consistent, it makes it much easier for both of us."

Tips for Managing Daily Routines

Tom, age 14, is making good progress in school, but he has trouble getting going in the morning. He often misses the school bus.

Juan, an energetic 8-year-old, has a hard time settling down at mealtimes. He keeps getting up from his chair to look out the window or pet the dog. When he does sit at the table, he often plays with his food or daydreams. Juan's parents have given up on trying to get him to eat with the rest of the family.

Nicole, age 12, is a seasoned veteran of the "Homework Wars." She's been fighting her parents on this front for years, yet it seems that nobody ever wins.

If any of this sounds familiar, you're not alone. Parents of children with ADHD struggle every day to keep their kids on schedule—whether it's getting ready for school, eating meals, doing homework, or going to bed. The following pages feature some of the ways you can work with your child to manage daily routines more successfully.

Managing Morning Madness

In most families, mornings are often pretty frantic, especially when parents and children need to get going early. In families with children who have ADHD, the usual morning madness can be magnified ten-fold. Children with ADHD may forget where they put their homework or gym shoes, dawdle over getting dressed, tie up the bathroom, and take what seems like forever to eat breakfast. The following tips may help you and your family bring some sanity to your morning routines.

• Allow enough time in the morning. Being rushed upsets everyone. If necessary, wake up your child earlier.

• Design a list of morning routine "must do" tasks in step-by-step order. Make copies of the list and have your child check off each task as it is completed.

For example:

Mike's Morning Routine

    ____**1. Get dressed before leaving your bedroom.**

    ____**2. Use the bathroom before coming downstairs.**

    ____**3. Feed the dog before eating breakfast.**

    ____**4. Eat breakfast before playing.**

Make the list more fun by using different designs, like a road map or race track.

- Arrange drawers and closets so your child can find school clothes quickly. Or, have your child select school clothes in the evening, to avoid the morning rush.

- Have your child put all of his or her homework and school supplies in the same place each night before going to bed. Place a box or basket near the door; it's easier to remember when it's in plain sight.

- Keep the TV turned off in the morning.

- Try to cut down on nagging and arguments. Notice and comment on what's been accomplished instead of focusing on what isn't done yet. Send your child off to school happy!

- Pick and choose your battles. Getting to the bus on time may be more important than combed hair.

Dealing with Dinner Disasters

Family mealtimes can be difficult under even the best of circumstances. When you have a child with ADHD, he or she can be very difficult to handle. The following ideas can help you manage mealtimes more effectively.

- Select the best time for medication doses. Try to time Ritalin or other medication doses so that they have the least effect on mealtime appetite.

- Encourage your child to stay at the table until he or she has finished eating. Once the child leaves the table, don't allow him or her to return. (You may want to give a warning as the child leaves: "Remember, if you leave the table now, you can't come back later.")

• Cut down on distractions. If the table is near a window, close the curtains during the meal. Keep the TV/radio off.

• Make meals fun. Every so often, have a "backwards" meal (start with dessert) or a "crazy" meal (pizza for breakfast, pancakes and eggs for dinner). It can break the pattern of mealtime struggles.

• Practice only one or two table manners at a time. Constant criticism during meals is no fun for anyone.

• Remember that sitting at the table is hard for kids with ADHD. Allow your child to leave the table as soon as he or she is finished eating, even if the rest of the family hasn't finished yet. Or give your child a chance to get up and move around—for example, by clearing the dishes before dessert is served.

Healing Homework Headaches

Many children dislike doing homework. Children with ADHD often get less done at school, so they may have even more homework than their peers. And because of their short attention spans, it may take them longer to finish homework. The following tips can help your child stay on task and finish homework with time to spare.

• Contact your child's teacher to work out a consistent system for communicating homework assignments. Ideally, the teacher will write the assignment on the board and make sure that your child records it correctly, in a special homework notebook, for example. You might also talk with the teacher about the amount of homework assigned if your child is having trouble finishing assignments. The teacher may be willing to assign fewer math or spelling problems for your child.

- Set up a quiet, comfortable place for your child to work. Make sure there's plenty of room to get up and move around. Some older kids like to read while pedaling an exercise bicycle. Other kids find it easier to memorize information while pacing around the study area.

- Establish a set time each day for homework. This might be right after school, or right after dinner. Let your child have a say about what time works best.

- Encourage your child to take breaks. He or she can finish a set amount of work, then take a "breather," then work again. Gradually increase the amount of work between breaks.

- Make a game of homework. If you think a task should take 10 minutes, set a timer for 20 minutes. Allow your child to "beat the clock."

- Be creative. Use a tape recorder, computer, flash cards, games—whatever works.

- Look for ways your child can succeed. For example, practice spelling 5 words instead of 10. Find fun and interesting ways to check your child's learning. Play the part of a famous person and "interview" your child about a historical or current event.

- Let your child play "teacher." Many children love to play teacher. Let your child give you (or a brother or sister) a spelling test. This allows your child to see, hear, and correct the words. Then it can be your turn to quiz the child.

- Hire a tutor, if financially possible. If your child is struggling to keep up in school or is having trouble with homework, a tutor can help. For some children with ADHD, tutoring provides the academic support necessary to prevent pulling them out of the classroom for one-on-one help.

- Talk with your doctor if your child is having trouble getting homework done. If your child is on medication, a dose late in the afternoon may help him or her focus on homework.

- Remember that you are the parent, not the teacher. Try to keep your teaching to a minimum. Offer your support, but don't do your child's homework.

Tips for Handling Birthdays and Holidays

Birthdays, holidays, and other major social events (such as weddings, family reunions) are stressful for most families. They can be even more stressful for families with a child who has ADHD. Much of this stress stems from the desire to celebrate an event as the "perfect family." The house must be perfectly decorated, the food must be perfectly cooked and served, the gifts must be perfect, and all family members must be happy and perfectly behaved. As most know, however, this perfect picture doesn't reflect reality, and someone is usually disappointed.

The following suggestions may help you and your family enjoy holidays and social events in a more relaxed and "hassle-free" atmosphere.

- Lower your expectations—and your family's. Instead of aiming for perfection, keep family celebrations simple. For major holidays, choose one or two activities that your children really enjoy, and leave it at that. Invite everyone to bake cookies, decorate the house or tree, wrap gifts, make cards, and so on—and don't worry if the results aren't perfect. If you find the preparations too stressful, skip the big holiday trip or house party and have a small family celebration instead.

•Play down the event or occasion, if possible. Many children with ADHD anticipate holidays and birthdays weeks or even months in advance, and may become anxious and tense about the upcoming event. If you can, avoid talking about the event too far ahead of time, and delay decorations or preparations until closer to the event. For example, decorate for a party the day before it.

•Stay calm and organized during holidays and social events. Eventually, your behavior will influence your children's behavior.

•Limit birthday choices. Instead of planning a large birthday party for your child, ask him or her to choose one or two friends to invite to lunch at a fast food restaurant, a children's matinee, or a trip to the zoo. Indoor playgrounds are also good choices for birthday parties because they provide a safe place for kids to burn off energy.

Giving Directions That Work
(or "When did you ask me to do that?")

Mary asked her 9-year-old son, Aaron, to put his bike in the garage before dinner. Twenty minutes later, as the rest of the family was sitting down to dinner, the bike was still in the driveway. Meanwhile, Aaron was busy gathering flowers from the neighbor's garden to decorate the table!

In addition to "Sit down" and "Be quiet," the words that children with ADHD hear most often are "This is the third (or fourth, or fifth) time I've asked you to..." Most of the time, these children don't ignore their parents' requests on purpose. Maybe they were thinking about something else, and didn't hear the request. Or maybe they started to hang up their jacket, but got side-tracked on the way to the closet.

Like most children, your child wants to please you and do things right. But because of ADHD, he or she may not hear—or remember—your directions. Your child may have a hard time staying on task long enough to finish chores. Some days, it may seem that the struggle to get chores done isn't worth the effort. Don't give up too soon, however. For any child, doing chores around the house is an important part of learning to be responsible.

The following tips can help your child follow directions and complete tasks more easily:

- Be sure that you have your child's attention before giving directions. Make eye contact or gently touch your child's shoulder to get his or her attention.

- Give one direction at a time. Instead of asking your child, "Please put your books away, get your sweater from the porch, and then come in for lunch," make just one request at a time. Then wait until the task is done before making the next request. And don't forget to be clear about when you want the task to be done!

- Use visual clues and gestures when you give directions. For some chores, you may need to show your child what you want him or her to do. For younger children, using a chart with pictures is a good way to remind them of what they need to do.

- Be prepared to say it again. You may need to state your request in a different way to make sure it is understood. Try to stay calm. Encourage your child to say, "Stop, I'm getting confused and I need to have you repeat that."

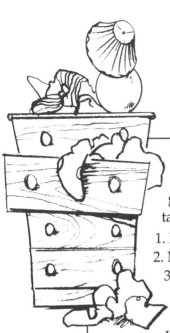

•Break a complex job into simpler tasks.
Instead of asking Joey to clean his room before going over to a friend's house, make a list of the tasks Joey needs to do:

1. Empty the wastebasket.
2. Make your bed.
3. Put your toys on the shelf.
4. Vacuum the rug.
5. Dust the dresser.

If you use a list, help your child think of the right order to do the tasks. Ask your child to read the list out loud and to check off each task as it is completed.

•Use a chart for daily chores. After finishing a chore, your child can put a star or sticker next to that task. At the end of the week, the stars or stickers can be traded for a reward.

•Work on developing your child's vocabulary to improve comprehension. Some children with ADHD have delayed language development, which makes it even harder for them to follow directions. If this is a problem for your child, try these ideas for improving vocabulary:

–Define and label objects frequently.

–Explain how objects are similar or different.

–Repeat a new word and its definition several times.

–Model the correct use of words when your child misuses them.

•Reward progress, not perfection. If you don't expect perfection, you won't be disappointed. Look instead for signs of progress, and give rewards and praise appropriate for your child's age. The rewards don't have to be tied to food or money. They can be gifts of time with people—such as an extra 10 minutes with Dad—a trip to the zoo, a game of catch in the park, renting a favorite video tape, or a walk in the neighborhood.

Exercises for Building Better Behavior

Children with ADHD often act or speak before thinking. This impulsive behavior, combined with their boundless energy, can make kids with ADHD difficult to be around.

Take the situation of 7-year-old Jesse. He loves to go to the playground with his parents and older brother. Jesse has energy to spare. He's also fearless, and takes chances that earn him lots of scrapes and bruises. He tends to push slower kids out of his way, and gets into arguments with other kids. His parents spend a lot of time saying, "Be careful," "Don't jump from there," and "Please don't push." Trips to the playground aren't't much fun for the rest of the family.

There are many things you can do to help your child build more positive behaviors. Behavior change takes time and hard work, but the reward is a happier child and a more peaceful home life. Be patient and stick with it!

- **Be firm when setting limits**. State rules clearly, and then refuse to argue with your child about them. Arguing will only encourage your child to push harder for control.

- **Reduce distractions** while your child is doing a chore or listening to directions. For example:

  –No TV or radio when doing homework

  –No pets in the bedroom while you are getting dressed

- **Develop a reward system to encourage positive behavior. Your child might earn a star for:**

  –Staying at the table during meals

  –Waiting for his or her turn during games

  –Not interrupting when you're on the phone

–Getting dressed without being reminded

–Controlling his or her behavior in public

At the end of the day, your child can turn in the stars for a small reward (an extra story at bedtime, for example). At the end of the week, the total "points" can be added up for a bigger reward.

- **Tell your child what TO DO, rather than what NOT to do**

Say:	Instead of:
Eat your dinner.	Stop daydreaming.
Wait your turn.	Don't interrupt.
Stop and look before crossing.	Don't run into the street.

- **Be positive.** Negative comments damage a child's self-esteem. Look for ways to compliment your child. Instead of saying, "It's about time you let someone else have a turn," try saying, "I'm glad you let your sister go first."

- **Empathize.** Let your child know that you recognize how difficult it is. Say something like, "I know it's really hard to sit still right now, but you can do it!"

- **Plan ahead.** It's hard for children with ADHD to wait for a table at a restaurant or sit quietly through a movie. A trip to the mall usually ends in tears or tantrums. By now, you know which situations are hard for your child. You may need to avoid some difficult situations for a while. For others, with a bit of advance planning, you can help your child avoid being uncontrollable. Following are a few ideas:

–Review the rules before entering public places so your child knows what to expect.

–Go to "family" restaurants or buffets, where a little noise doesn't bother other diners. Try to beat the rush so you won't have to wait for a table.

–Bring small toys, puzzles, or paper and crayons to keep your child busy while waiting for food to be served in a restaurant. Older children may enjoy a hand-held computer game or a book while waiting. Bring a healthy snack along in case your child gets hungry.

–Plan for shorter trips to the store. That way, you can help your child be successful in public places.

–If you have a VCR, rent a video instead of going to a movie theater. When you do go to the theater, take your child out for several breaks during the show.

–Plan outings that involve physical activity, like picnics, hiking, camping, or biking. Then your child can be active and noisy without bothering others.

–Avoid planning events when your child is likely to be overly tired. In children with ADHD, fatigue often increases negative behaviors.

• **Work on improving behavior** in areas in which you know your child can succeed. For example:

–Ask your child to pick up blocks, rather than clean the entire playroom.

–Ask your child to sit at the table for five more minutes (you can set a timer), rather than sit through the entire meal.

• **Teach your child how to slow down.** Help your child learn to STOP, RELAX, and THINK. Having your child take deep breaths is a good way to slow down. So is encouraging your child to take a break.

• **Provide consistent routines.** Your child may function best when following set routines. For example:

1. Brush your teeth.
2. Wash your face.
3. Use the toilet.
4. Put on your pajamas.
5. Pick out a bedtime story.

• **Use private visual or physical cues as reminders.** These cues can communicate without embarrassing your child. A thumbs-up sign or a gentle touch on the shoulder can mean "slow down." A wink can mean "please be quiet." Raised eyebrows can mean "please stop and think first." Cue words might be "think," "wait," or a nonsense word that has a special meaning for your child.

Using Positive Discipline

Disciplining children who have ADHD is a special challenge for many parents. Children with ADHD are typically not rule-bound, nor do they have a lot of respect for authority. They may not have a strong sense of boundaries—their own or others'—and they tend to be very persistent. Add to this the fact that these children don't seem to learn from their mistakes, and you have a recipe for a disciplinary nightmare.

The next time your child breaks a rule or behaves inappropriately, try this three-step approach to positive discipline:

1. **Give a warning.** Restate the rule and the consequence for breaking the rule: "If you do x, you choose the consequence of y."

2. **Deliver the consequence.** If your child continues the behavior, deliver the consequence. The consequence should be brief and non-shaming, such as a time-out or a withdrawal of privileges. Examples include turning off the TV if the child refuses to come to the table for dinner, or a 10-minute time-out for hitting a sibling.

3. **Use the discipline as a teaching tool.** Don't just end with the punishment. Instead, ask your child to think of a better choice, and say that you'll watch for the improved behavior.

Because children with ADHD need social interaction with their peers, avoid using social isolation as a consequence of misbehavior—such as, "If you don't clean your room, you can't have Teddy over to play this weekend". Find other "incentives" to encourage good behavior, such as special time together that is meaningful to your family—biking, playing at the park, rollerblading, or going to a baseball game.

Helping Siblings Cope with ADHD

It's tough to be the brother or sister of a child with ADHD. Children may be easily embarrassed by the antics of their ADHD sibling, and may resent all of the time and attention this child receives. Add to this the fact that the child with ADHD tends to be loud, disruptive, and invasive of siblings' privacy. Here are some steps you can take to help your other child/children cope with their "difficult" sibling:

•**Spend time alone with your other child(ren).** Set aside time each week to spend some quiet time or do something fun with your non-ADHD children. Get a babysitter, and go out to dinner, a movie, a concert, or the amusement park to give your other children a break.

•**Help your other children understand ADHD.** Your children may be more tolerant and understanding of their sibling's behavior if they know more about ADHD and its symptoms.

•**Find acceptable ways to deal with ADHD behavior.** Having a sibling with ADHD can be very embarrassing, especially for older children. When you are planning a family outing, talk about expectations for behavior. Do some role playing and problem solving with your children (including your child with ADHD) to identify acceptable ways of dealing with embarrassing behaviors.

•**Reduce chances for embarrassment.** Avoid taking your child with ADHD to fancy restaurants or to places that require silence (concerts, movies, or plays). Get a sitter for these events, and be sure to provide something fun and interesting (such as a new toy or game) for your stay-at-home child to do during the family's absence.

- **Look for ADHD resources** that will help your non-ADHD children learn about ADHD and how to cope with it. Several books for children are listed in Chapter 7.

Tips for Frazzled Parents

Being the parent of a child with ADHD can be a challenge, to say the least—especially for those parents who have ADHD themselves. If your child is very active and noisy, you may be tired much of the time. If your child is having trouble in school, you have something extra to worry about. Everything seems to take longer with a child who has ADHD. To be the best parent you can, you need to take care of yourself, too. Following are some ideas that can help:

- **Ask for help from friends and relatives.** "Help" can be emotional or physical. You'll need advice and a listening ear from time to time, not to mention a break. Find a friend or relative who will take care of your child for an evening or a weekend so you can "get away from it all."

- **Get help from professionals.** Call your child's doctor or therapist if you're having trouble coping. Read books or take classes to learn more about ADHD. (Chapter 7 of this guide lists resources that can help you and your child manage ADHD more effectively.)

- **Join a support group** to meet other parents of children with ADHD. In a parent support group, you'll learn that you're not alone—other parents are also struggling with the fears, worries, and frustrations of parenting a child with ADHD.

You can share your stories with people who understand, get tips on effective behavior-management strategies, and learn how to be an advocate for your child.

- **Stay in close contact** with your child's teachers and other school personnel. You'll need their help and support, and they'll need yours. Plan to meet with your child's teacher regularly to talk about your child's needs and progress in school.

- **Remember to enjoy your child.** This isn't always easy, especially when you've had a bad day. Take a few minutes to laugh about something your child has said or done. Take a walk around the block, or go for a car ride. Sing your child's favorite song. Let the worries slide for awhile, and just focus on having fun.

- **Focus on your child's positive behaviors.** No one likes to have their faults pointed out repeatedly. Try to "catch your child at being good" and comment on what they do well. In fact, look for behaviors that are just "OK" and talk about it. You will feel better about your child, and your child will feel better, too.

Building Better Behavior

By nature, children with ADHD are impulsive. They have a hard time seeing another person's point of view, they tend to blame others for their problems, and they don't always take responsibility well. The following section presents some exercises that you and your child can use to build better behavior.

Using a Picture Point System

For a younger child, use a picture to symbolize the reward for positive behavior. When the picture is completed, the child gets the reward. Here are some examples:

Every time I set the table without being asked twice, I get to fill in a circle on the ice cream cone. When all the circles are full, I get an ice cream cone!

Every time I remember to take my homework to school, I can connect another dot. When the picture is done, we're going to the zoo!

Using a Point System

A point system can work for children at any age, as long as the behaviors and rewards are appropriate for the child's age. Here's an example of eight-year-old Kari's point system:

Kari earns points for: # of points

Getting out of bed without help.................................... 1

Being ready for school on time........................ 1

Getting no behavior slips
at school today.. 3

Feeding the dog each morning.......................... 2

Doing 30 minutes of homework 3

Kari's points earn her:

1/2 hour of TV 3

1 hour of TV 6

Video movie on weekend 30

Game time with Mom or Dad 6

Staying up late on
Friday night.................................30

You may want to purchase an all-purpose chart that uses erasable markers. Older children can use this type of chart to check off their tasks and keep track of their points.

Using Behavioral Contracts

Behavioral contracts seem to work especially well for young teenagers as long as the expected behaviors are clearly defined. Signing a contract gives teenagers an added sense of responsibility. Here's an example of a contract to reduce argumentative behavior:

Kevin's Contract

Every time I do my homework without arguing, I will earn 50¢.

Date: _____

Signed: _____
(Child)

Signed: _____
(Parent)

Whichever system you decide to use, be sure to keep it simple, understandable, and workable for you and your child.

Problem Solving Made Easier

Knowing how to solve problems is a skill that will serve your child well. Here's a process that Susan uses to help her 10-year-old daughter, Angie, solve her own problems.

Solving Problems—

 1. **STOP:** Slow down... **Take a deep breath.**

 2. **THINK:** **What is my problem?** Mom won't let me go outside until I finish the dishes.

 3. **OPTIONS:** **What are my choices?**

I could go outside anyway.

I could have a tantrum.

What might happen if I do each of these things?

The dishes will get done and Mom will be happy.

I could do what Mom wants.

I could hit her or call her names.

Mom will be mad and I could get grounded.

I might have to spend time in my room until I calm down.

 4. **PLAN:** **What am I going to do? How did I do?** Is this a good plan? ___ Yes ___ No How did my plan work?

Practice these steps on little problems first, like whether or not to eat breakfast. Then try it out on bigger problems. For parents of teenagers, it's a good idea to practice using the process with your child on a "what if?" basis: What if you decide to break curfew? What if your friends dare you to use drugs, or to steal something? You can play "devil's advocate" and point out the negative things that could happen for each choice. Let your child come up with the positive ones. Then reverse the roles for a different problem and let your child point out the negatives, while you point out the positives. This problem-solving role playing is good practice.

You may want to make copies of the Problem-Solving Worksheet on the next page. Give your child a few copies to practice solving problems on paper.

Some of these tools will work better for your child than others. Try them out, and use the ones that work the best for your situations. Remember that your efforts will pay off over time. Be patient!

STOP Problem-Solving Worksheet

 1. STOP: Slow down... Take a deep breath.

2. THINK: What is my problem?

_____

_____

3. OPTIONS: What are my choices?

_____

_____

What might happen if I do each of these things?

_____

_____

4. PLAN: What am I going to do?

_____

_____

How did I do? _____

_____

Is this a good plan? _____ Yes _____ No
How did my plan work?

_____

_____

Especially for Teens: Living with ADHD at Home

- Remember that almost all teens have some trouble getting along with their parents. It's a natural part of growing up.

- Work with your parents to set goals that are important to you. You'll probably need to negotiate and compromise.

- If you don't understand your parents' rules, ask them to explain them again, or to write the rules down. Ask if you can have a say in setting the rules.

- Teens with ADHD are at greater risk for behavior problems than other teens. This means you'll have to work extra hard at keeping your cool at home.

- Try using a "time planner" to plan your homework schedule each evening. For example, you'll do your math assignment from 7:00 to 7:30, and your English assignment from 7:30 to 8:30. A time planner is also a great tool for making sure that term papers get completed on time.

- Your ADHD might lead you to make snap decisions without thinking them through first. Try using the STOP...THINK problem-solving process to make decisions about problems you are facing.

- Remember that more privileges mean greater responsibility. If you want more freedom, you need to show your parents that you can handle it.

- If you're working on improving a behavior, write a contract with yourself to help you stick with it. Ask your parents if they will reward you for reaching your goal.

- If you have a big or important decision to make, give yourself 24 hours to think about it before deciding. Waiting may help you be less emotional to make a better decision.

"When the teacher yells at you, BE QUIET!"

Nate, 4th grader

Isaiah, who just started fifth grade, is having trouble finishing his homework. It's not that he isn't trying—he just can't remember the assignments. Isaiah's mother called his teacher to discuss the problem. His teacher suggested that Isaiah use a notebook just for homework assignments. Each subject in the notebook has a different colored tab to make it easier for Isaiah to find the right place. Isaiah's teacher is willing to repeat directions if he doesn't understand them. This system is working well so far.

Because children with ADHD have trouble focusing on one thing at a time, they often have problems in school. Many children with ADHD also have some type of learning disability, which can compound the problem. While children with ADHD have to work harder than their peers to do well in school, they can succeed. This chapter presents tips for parents, teachers, and children to help your child to do better in school.

Tips for Parents

John's parents were at their wits' ends. John brought home another note from his teacher—the third one in two weeks! This time, John had disrupted the class by talking out of turn and leaving his seat several times. When his teacher asked him to sit down, he talked back. John's parents met with his teacher and together they worked out a system to reward better behavior in class. John still acts out now and then, but he's improving. Believe it or not, there are a lot of things you can do to help your child do better in school. First and foremost, it's important for you to be a strong advocate for your child. Most schools offer several services to help children with learning difficulties. These services vary, depending on the child's needs and problems. You are encouraged to talk with school personnel to explore all possible services available to your child.

Following are some additional ideas to help your child succeed in school:

- **Notify your child's teacher** that he or she has ADHD (or ADD), if you haven't already done so. A sample letter to teachers is presented at the end of this chapter. It's important for teachers to know:

  –What ADHD is, and your child's main symptoms

  –Whether your child is taking medication, and when it should be given

  –What the teacher can do to help your child do better in school

  –That you are willing to work with the teacher to help your child succeed

- **Meet with your child's teacher** early in each new school year. Discuss special behavior or learning problems and work out a management plan. Ask about the best way to communicate your child's needs and get feedback from the teacher.

- **Establish a good working relationship** with your child's teacher. Keep in close contact with the teacher and other school personnel during the school year, and offer to work with them to prevent problems.

- **Be sure to notify the teacher/school** if your child's medication changes.

- **Inform the teacher of any major changes at home.** Let your child's teacher know of any major changes in your child's home life, such as an upcoming move, a new baby, a separation or divorce, or a parent being out of work. These kinds of changes can be especially hard for children with ADHD.

- **Work with your child to cut down on homework hassles.** Chapter 3 in this guidebook presents ways you can help your child get homework done on time.

- **Request that the school identify learning disabilities** as early as possible. About 40 percent of children with ADHD have learning disabilities. If your child is one of them, get help from a professional. And be sure to let your child's teacher know how he or she can help.

- **Discuss next year's teacher assignment** with the principal. Describe your child's needs and emphasize the importance of a good student-teacher match up.

- **If you have a bad experience with one teacher, stay positive.** Not all experiences will be negative, and your child needs you to remain optimistic.

- **If your child has ADHD but does not qualify for special education services, talk to the teachers about other options.**

- **Be your child's advocate.** Remember, you are the best and perhaps the only advocate your child has. Don't be afraid to ask for what you need.

Some teachers are well-informed about ADHD, while others are not so informed. The tips on the following pages are addressed to teachers. You may want to photocopy these pages and share them with your child's teacher.

Tips for Teachers

Whether you knew it or not, you've probably had children with ADHD in your class before. They're the ones who can't seem to sit still, who answer questions without raising their hands, who talk when they should be listening. They're the daydreamers and the "class clowns." They're the ones who often forget their homework or turn in incomplete assignments. Of course, any child can do a few of these things and not have ADHD. Children with ADHD, on the other hand, may do all of them.

Teaching children with ADHD can be very challenging and very frustrating. But, with a better understanding of ADHD and a few "tricks," you can help your students with ADHD to increase their successes in the classroom. You can also cut down on the amount of disruptive behavior that is common with these children. Try the following suggestions with your students who have ADHD:

- **Realize that children with ADHD are just as intelligent** and creative as the other children in your class. Children with ADHD are often highly intelligent, but they do have trouble organizing and processing information. They also have a difficult time sitting still and paying attention, so they may miss the main point of the lesson.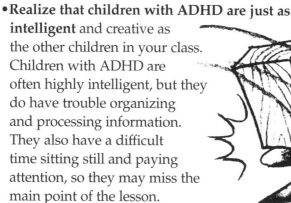

- **Avoid using negative labels.** Many children with ADHD are underachievers. As a result, they are often mislabeled as "lazy" or "unmotivated." It's important to distinguish inattentiveness from lack of motivation.

- **Encourage participation.** Children with ADHD can be enthusiastic about learning. Give them opportunities to help and participate actively in the classroom.

- **Separate work into small chunks.** Children can complete each task and then move on to the next one without getting confused. This approach also gives children a sense of accomplishment.

- **Set up structured times** for classroom study, to better manage noise and other distractions. Provide additional structure in the form of clear communications of expectations, rules, consequences, and follow-up.

- **Experiment to find the best seating** location, in order to cut down on visual distractions. For example, seat the child near the front of the room and away from the window.

- **Write assignments on the board.** In addition to giving verbal assignments, be sure to write them on the chalkboard or hand them out in written form. Break complex assignments into smaller steps.

- **Suggest homework notebooks or accordion folders** for

children with ADHD. When children put their assignments in the same place each time, they have less chance of losing them or forgetting the details.

- **Encourage students to ask for clarification** if they don't understand a concept or rule, or if they are confused about directions. Children should feel comfortable asking for help.

- **Allow students with ADHD extra time for tests.** They may also need to take tests in a supervised place that is free from distractions.

- **Give rewards often while a child is on task.** For younger children, these rewards can be a sticker, a privilege, or verbal praise. For most older students, your quiet recognition of a job well done can be motivating, yet not embarrassing.

- **Talk about your students' good points.** Children with ADHD need a lot of encouragement and self-esteem boosters.

- **Use multimedia materials** to engage students' interest and attention. These materials can be audio-or videotapes, calculators, computers, games, costumes, or memory joggers.

- **Allow your students with ADHD to use alternative ways of sharing information.** Students who have trouble with written assignments could be encouraged to use a word processor, share information orally, or dictate their answers on audio cassette tape.

- **Build in times to get up and move around,** especially for younger children. Children with ADHD need to move. Every chance they have to release energy—without getting into trouble—will help them settle in for the next task. A trip to the library, a walk outside to look at the spring buds, a chance to act out a story, or to stand up while working on assignments—whenever you can combine learning with movement, you'll be doing these children a big favor.

- **Teach the child** to monitor his or her own level of "on-task" behavior.

- **Prepare students with ADHD for transitional times and changes in routine.** Children with ADHD handle transitions and changes much better when they know about them ahead of time. Let your students know when a change will happen, why, and what they can expect.

- **Try to remain calm,** even when the child's behavior is very disruptive. High risk times for these children tend to be unstructured periods like lunch and recess. Try to plan ahead for problem situations, and keep your cool!

- **Identify one or two negative behaviors to work on at a time.** Trying to work on too many things at once will only confuse the child. Focus on teaching desirable behaviors, rather than eliminating undesirable ones.

- **Share positive observations** about the child's behavior, along with your concerns, when communicating with parents.

- **Provide immediate consequences whenever possible.** If children fail to follow rules, requests or limits, respond immediately.

- **ADHD is a disability and will affect children to varying degrees.** It may be necessary to talk to the class about how ADHD affects children. Do this with out naming any child in particular.

- **Use charts and contracts.** Children with ADHD may behave best when they use charts or contracts that reinforce and reward their behavior.

- **Use response-cost/behavior penalty systems.** With this system, a child a child learns a pre-determined number of points or tokens to get a reward. Inappropriate behavior results in loss of points. In this way, the child is motivated to keep the points.

- **Use charts and contracts.** Children with ADHD may behave best when they use charts or contracts that reinforce and reward their behavior.

- **Be aware of noise.** Some children are very distracted by noise in the classroom. Consider allowing children to use headphones to listen to quiet music or "white noise" while they are working.

What Parents Should Know

The following "advice to parents" was provided by teachers who have taught students with ADHD.

A Message from Teachers to Parents

- It's important for us to get to know you and your child. That way, you can tell us your needs and expectations, and we can tell you what we need to help your child succeed in school.

- Your child is responsible for schoolwork and assignments.

- You are always welcome to see your child in the school.

- A weekly call to "check in" on your child's progress is appreciated.

- Your child should be allowed to experience the consequences of his or her actions.

- A child with ADHD takes extra time and effort in the classroom. Your child can't always get our full attention.

- A yearly update from your child's doctor regarding medication is a must.

- We need a backup plan in case your child forgets to bring medication to school.

Tips for Students

Oh, oh—not another behavior slip from my teacher! What did I do this time? Maybe I can "lose" it on the way home.... Or I can tell Dad it was all LeRoy's fault. He might actually believe it this time.

As you probably know, children with ADHD often get into trouble with their teachers. They interrupt when their teacher is talking, or they get up from their chairs when they shouldn't. Sometimes they don't finish their homework because they forgot what they were supposed to do. You might do a few of these things yourself.

Some of the following ideas can help you do better in school. Try them out and see which ones work for you.

- **Identify behaviors or situations that are problems for you,** and ask your parents and teachers for suggestions that might help.

- **Set goals you know you can reach.** This might take some practice. Be realistic and work on one goal at a time.

- **Build routines for yourself.** Maybe you like to do your homework right after school and get it out of the way. Or maybe you need a break when you get home, and find it easier to do schoolwork after dinner. You might study best when you move around, or when it's completely quiet. Try different things, and use the ones that work best for you.

- **Use a notebook to write your assignments** in so you won't forget them.

- **Take a break** after you've done a set amount of homework. Get up, move around, go get a soda, take the dog for a short walk—whatever you need to do so you can settle down to do your next assignment.

- **Give yourself a reward** when you reach your goals. For example, finishing and turning in all of your homework for one week might earn you a trip to the arcade, a movie, a new CD, or whatever suits you and your parents.

- **Set short-term goals for long assignments.** It's easy to put off working on an assignment that isn't due until next week. Resist the urge. Write your short-term goals in your assignment notebook or time planner. Then try to do a little each day, so you won't have to cram it all in the night before the project is due.

- **Try putting a penny or a paper clip in your pocket** if you have trouble sitting still in class. Fiddling with this object might help you sit still and pay attention in class.

- **Learn how to relax.** Taking long, slow, deep breaths can help you relax when you're feeling anxious or fidgety. Closing your eyes and imagining yourself in a favorite place is also a good way to relax.

- **Practice the STOP...THINK problem-solving strategy,** especially when you feel frustrated.

- **Know why you are taking medication.** If you are taking medication, learn as much as you can about it. Realize that taking medication is similar to wearing glasses: It helps bring your brain into focus so you can pay attention better.

- **Remember that having ADHD** has nothing to do with how smart you are. Kids who have ADHD are just as smart as other kids; they just have trouble focusing energy. You may have to work harder to sit still and concentrate.

- **Learn about your strengths and weaknesses.** Be proud of what you're good at and enjoy doing. And work on turning your weaknesses into strengths. If you have trouble remembering, use "memory joggers." Place a box or basket near the door to put your homework in each night; this will help you remember to take it to school. Making a list of the things you need to do, and then checking off each item as you go, can also be a big help.

- **Get involved in physical activities**. Choose something you enjoy. Some students do best in non-competitive sports, like swimming, karate, or gymnastics. Tennis, track, or soccer can also be good choices.

- **Don't give up.** Sometimes you might have to work harder than your friends to do well in school or in a job, but keep trying. Your hard work will pay off!

Sample Letter for Teachers

The following represents a sample letter to inform teachers that a student has ADHD. Feel free to modify this letter and use it to communicate with your child's teacher.

Dear _____,

My child, _____, has been diagnosed as having attention deficit hyperactivity disorder (ADHD). ADHD is a neurodevelopmental disorder that affects my child's ability to sit still and concentrate for long periods of time.

My child's ADHD symptoms include:

• Having a difficult time sitting still

• Having trouble remembering spoken directions

• Being easily distracted

• Having trouble adjusting to new situations

• Other: _____

_____

Certain types of medication can help children with ADHD to calm down and focus their attention.

My child is taking _____ .

This medication needs to be taken during the school day

at_____(time). I have already talked with the school nurse about medication, but you may need to help my child remember to go to the nurse's office on time.

I would like to meet with you to talk about ways we can work together to maximize my child's classroom behavior and ability to learn. I have some ideas that may help with behavior management. I would also like to hear your ideas about what we can do at home, in order to help get school assignments completed on time. I will call you soon to set up an appointment.

Sincerely,

Especially for Teens: Living with ADHD at School

- Be an advocate for yourself. If you need it, ask for extra time to take tests. Ask for help whenever—and as often as—you feel you need it. You deserve extra help if you need it!

- If your memory skills are weak, it's OK to write things down. Become an expert note taker!

- If your handwriting or written language skills are weak, learn to use the computer.

- If you have a hard time taking notes, use a tape recorder for important lectures and assignments.

- Keep your daily assignment notebook or folder up-to-date. Work hard to keep up with your homework. Uncompleted assignments can really lower your grades.

- Build extra time into your schedule (like study halls) to give yourself more time to finish your work at school.

- Exercise your independence by taking charge of your homework. Try to get it done on your own, without being nagged by adults.

- Remember that medication may help you focus and maintain your attention, but it won't do your homework for you!

- Recognize your strengths and your weaknesses. Appreciate your strengths, and work on improving the areas in which you're weak.

- Keep your sense of humor, and build good relationships with your teachers.

- Remember: You're just as smart as the next person (if not smarter). You just have to work a little harder to make it known!

"With my medication, *I'm 120% better–
I can do my schoolwork, think better, and get
along with my friends."*

—Shay, age 17

When Rochelle was a toddler, the other kids at day care steered clear of her. She pushed, pinched, yelled, and grabbed their toys. By the time she was five years old, she had been in four different day care centers. When she started school, Rochelle's parents decided to take some steps to help her get along better with her peers. They signed her up for swimming lessons and T-ball. They invited one of her classmates over for a few hours on Saturday afternoon. They had a picnic and invited a neighbor child. Rochelle is still bossy and a bit pushy, but she's gradually learning how to be a good friend.

Many children with ADHD have a difficult time making friends and being team players. By nature, they are overactive, talkative, and impulsive. They sometimes say or do things that can be hurtful to others. They tend to "run wild" at friends' houses. They may be noisy in restaurants and theaters. Having few friends and few places where they can just "be themselves," these children often have low self-esteem. Low self-esteem makes it even more difficult for children with ADHD to fit in with their peers and handle social settings.

Following are tips for everyone who cares for children with ADHD. These can be used to help build self-esteem, learn social skills, and find an outlet for their energy in sports and other activities.

Building Self-Esteem

Children with ADHD hear some of these things almost every day:

"Hurry up and get ready. You're going to be late for school again."

"Don't spill your milk."

"Be quiet."

"Sit down and stay there!"

"Leave me alone."

"Pay attention."

"Get back to work."

"You forgot your homework again?"

"Quit bugging your sister."

"Stop pushing!"

And on and on. How would you feel if you had to listen to this all day long? It's not surprising that many children who have ADHD don't feel very good about themselves!

Parents often say these things in anger, without thinking. (And no wonder—being the parent of a child with ADHD can be frustrating and exhausting.) But teachers, relatives, and friends also say them. To help build your child's self-esteem, work on controlling what you say and educate others about which words and strategies are helpful in managing your child's behavior. The following tips can help.

- **Tell your child what TO DO**, instead of what NOT to do. State your wishes in a positive way. Say, "Sit on your chair" instead of "Stop getting up." Say "Please use your fork" instead of "Don't eat with your fingers."

- **Talk about your child's good points—often.** Use lots of affirming statements with your child. Say things like:

  -I love you just the way you are.

-I love your energy.

-I enjoy your sense of humor.

-I really like the way you shared with your friend.

-I was so glad to see you taking turns on the swings.

-You're a terrific artist.

-You did a great job cleaning your room.

Hearing positive statements like these—instead of constant nagging and criticism—can really boost your child's self-esteem.

•**Help your child succeed.** Let your child choose a sport or hobby that he or she enjoys. Get involved by helping your child practice and improve their chance of success. Praise successes and downplay failures.

There's nothing like success to build self-esteem: *Success + Success + Success = Self-confidence = Self-esteem!*

•**Encourage your child to be responsible** by expecting him or her to help with chores. Responsibility leads to feelings of competence.

•**Help your child master new skills and overcome fears.** Encourage your child to try new things to stretch his or her abilities. Don't push—just provide support.

•**Consider individual counseling to help** your child learn coping techniques, problem-solving strategies, and ways to deal with stress and low self-esteem.

Building Social Skills

Children with ADHD can have trouble getting along with their peers–even though they may be very friendly. Sometimes their high energy levels just wear out other children.

Children with ADHD may have a difficult time sharing or taking turns, respecting another child's boundaries, or understanding another's point of view. They may try to be bossy or take over an activity. They may not be aware of how others are reacting to their behavior.

The good news is that they can learn social skills to help them get along better with their friends. Here are some tips to help improve your child's social skills:

- **Practice eye contact.** Have your child practice looking at other people when he or she is talking to them.

- **Practice body language.** Have your child watch other people. Talk with your child about what people's body language and facial expressions are saying.

- **Practice social skills.** Role play with your child. Pretend you are a friend of your child's, and let him or her call you on the phone (for instance, to ask you to go to a movie).

- **Be a good role model.** Use good manners when talking to others. Your child may follow your example.

- **Use secret cues.** Your child may need help while practicing good manners. Agree on a few gestures, such as a wink, to remind them to say thank you.

- **Keep a sense of humor.** When giving your child feedback, make it fun. Playing with friends is supposed to be enjoyable!

Building Better Behavior

Children with ADHD tend to be impulsive. They react quickly, have a hard time seeing another person's point of view, blame others for their problems, and may have a hard time being responsible. In addition, children with ADHD may have trouble learning from their experiences. These difficulties can lead to repeated failures, continued frustration and discouragement. The following section presents some exercises that you and your child can use to build better behavior.

Using Token Systems

A token system is a behavior program where a child earns a point, chip or some other token for acceptable behavior and loses the token for unacceptable behavior. The tokens can be used to get rewards and privileges that you and your child have chosen together. Here are some tips on using token systems.

- **Consider your child's age.** Young children need rewards more often. Rewards may need to be given once or twice a day.

- **Make a wish list.** Rewards should be something that the child wants and that you can give within a short period of time.

- **Use tokens for specific behaviors.** Use tokens to change specific behavior so that your child will know exactly what to practice. You can stop using the tokens once the behavior has become a habit.

- **Change rewards often.** To keep the program interesting, you may need to change the rewards or the number of tokens required to get the reward.

- **Follow through on your reward commitments.** Success with tokens requires consistency and good follow-through.

- **Establish a system for taking tokens away.** After the child has learned to earn tokens, he or she can be "fined" or lose tokens for inappropriate behavior. This is called "response cost," which means, "If you misbehave, it will cost you."

When used correctly, the token system can be a win-win situation for you and your child. You get what you want (better behavior), and your child can earn a reward for doing it.

Playing Sports: What Your Child Should Know

Sports and other physical activities—such as biking, rollerblading, dancing, and swimming—are great ways for any child to release energy and tension. They also improve physical health, and give kids a chance to learn discipline and cooperation. The following tips will help your child choose—and do well in—any sport or activity.

- **Consider the following questions** when helping your child choose a sport:

  -Has my child failed at certain sports in the past? Which ones, and why?

  -How does my child spend his or her free time?

  -What type of activity does my child prefer? Working and playing individually, or as a part of a team?

  -How good are my child's hand-eye coordination, running skills, speed, endurance, and strength?

  -How mature is my child physically and emotionally?

  -How does my child cope in group activities?

  Use your answers to these questions as a guide to help your child choose a sport.

- **Consider team versus individual sports.** Some children with ADHD don't perform well in team sports. They may have trouble following directions, or get distracted by too much noise and activity. Others can't handle being teased or criticized by their coach or teammates. If your child has not done well in team sports, consider dance, karate, swimming, gymnastics, tennis, or track.

- **Try soccer.** If your child wants to try a team sport, soccer may be a good choice. Soccer involves a lot of running and kicking.

Everyone on the team gets a chance to play, and even less coordinated children can do fairly well.

- **Talk with the coach.** Talking with the coach before the program begins will ensure that your child's behavior is not misread as rudeness or disobedience.

- **Consider karate or tae kwon do.** These sports can be especially good for children with ADHD because they teach self-discipline and concentration. New techniques are not taught until students have learned to stop, listen, and think. If your child is interested in this type of sport, stress that what is learned should never be used in aggressive play. (Children who are unusually aggressive may not be good candidates for karate or tae kwon do. Be sure to talk in advance with the teacher about his or her philosophy.)

- **Realize that medication can improve sports participation.** If your child takes ADHD medication, there's a good chance that it can improve his or her ability to learn a sport and pay attention during games. Your child may have all of the physical skills for success, but be unable to concentrate on playing the game.

What Your Child Should Know About ADHD

The following information can help your child understand ADHD. Older children can read it themselves, and use the information to explain ADHD to others.

Especially for Kids: Living with ADHD

- ADHD is not a disease—it's the way your brain works.

- When the attention control center in your brain is weak, it's said that you have attention deficit disorder.
  - Attention means "being able to listen and concentrate."
  - Deficit means "not enough of."
  - Disorder means "not working right."

- When you have trouble sitting still and need to move around a lot, we say that you are hyperactive. Hyper means "too much."

- You were born with ADHD, and you will probably always have some problems with it. But you can learn ways to improve your attention.

- Having ADHD doesn't mean you're dumb or stupid. It has nothing to do with how smart you are.

- Having ADHD doesn't mean you're bad or naughty. Sometimes, it's just hard to stop and think long enough to make good choices—even though you want to.

- Some kids take medicine to help them control ADHD. The medicine goes to the attention control center in the brain and helps it work better.

- Taking medicine for ADHD is like wearing glasses: It helps focus your brain!

- Even though you have ADHD, there are many things that you're good at. There are also some things you may not be so good at—like listening or remembering directions. Enjoy the things you're good at, and work hard on improving your weaknesses. You can do it!

Especially for Teens: Living with ADHD

- ADHD is not a disease—it's the way your brain works.

- Your ADHD may not go away, but you can learn coping skills for areas where you're weak. Recognize your strengths and work hard to improve weaknesses.

- Hyperactivity may decrease as you get older, but you might still be more restless and fidgety than your peers.

- Your parents and teachers have higher expectations for your behavior than they did when you were younger. They may be less tolerant of impulsive or inattentive behavior.

- Your ADHD may lead you to make quick decisions without thinking them through. To avoid making decisions you'll regret later, use the STOP...THINK problem-solving process.

- Using medication to control ADHD does not increase your risk for using drugs. However, you should not experiment with drugs.

- Never adjust your medication yourself. Call your doctor. And never use other drugs with your medication, unless they are prescribed by your doctor.

- Medication for ADHD may actually reduce the anxiety, depression, and low self-esteem that some teenagers experience.

- If you are having problems with school, friends, or your family, this is NOT a good time to stop your medication.

- As you get older, your schoolwork will get more complex and challenging. You may have to learn new "tricks" to help you concentrate, get organized, and stay with your projects until they're done. Chapter 7 lists several books that can help you cut down on homework hassles.

- If your ADHD was diagnosed late, you may have some gaps in your learning. You might need some extra tutoring to catch up. An alternative school, where you can start fresh with teachers and peers, could also be helpful.

- Get the help you need—from teachers, doctors, therapists and, most of all—from your parents. You deserve it.

What Are You Good At?

Having ADHD means that you have trouble in some areas—like remembering directions and paying attention—but there are lots of things you're good at, too.

Pretend the drawing below is your brain. The large box is your attention control center. It's supposed to help you sit still and pay attention, but it doesn't always work as well as it should. The stars are the things you're good at. The squares are the things that are hard for you to do.

1. Next to each star, write something you're good at.

2. Next to each square, write something you're not so good at.

3. Below each square, write one thing you can do to improve. If you have trouble thinking of something, ask your mom or dad to help.

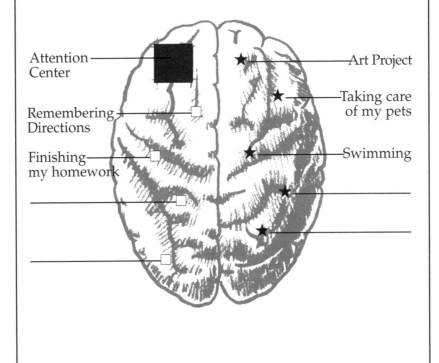

Attention Center

Remembering Directions

Finishing my homework

Art Project

Taking care of my pets

Swimming

C hildren with ADHD have now been followed into their adulthood. ADHD is a disability and can have different levels of severity. No two children are alike, and no one will have exactly the same problems. However, children with ADHD may experience some common problems as they grow.

What Research Tells Us

- **ADHD continues into adolescence and adulthood.** About seven out of 10 children diagnosed with ADHD as children will still meet diagnostic criteria at age 15. About five out of 10 will still have ADHD as adults.

- **Adolescents with ADHD have a higher rate of traffic accidents than those without ADHD.** They are also more likely to drive without a license, speed while driving, and have more injuries related to car accidents.

Chapter 6

Living with ADHD in Young Adulthood

- **ODD and CD lead to more behavior problems.** Adolescents with ADHD who also have oppositional defiant disorder (ODD) or conduct disorder (CD) have more long-lasting problems than those with ADHD only.

- **Cigarettes, alcohol and drugs are used more often by adolescents who have ADHD and CD.**

- **Academic difficulties are more common in adolescents with ADHD.** Learning disabilities, failing a grade level and being suspended from school also occur more often.

- **Family conflict is more common in families with a child with ADHD.** This conflict may be related to the school, behavioral, and parenting problems associated with raising children with ADHD.

While these statistics should be of concern to parents and teachers, not all children with ADHD experience these difficulties. Awareness of these problems helps reinforce the notion that we must do everything possible to help children with ADHD.

Here's some good news related to the outcomes of children with ADHD.

- **Higher intelligence results in better school outcomes** than low intelligence.

- **Higher family income results in better overall outcomes for children with ADHD**—perhaps because these families are more able to get the help they need.

- **Children with better social skills have fewer problems with interpersonal relationships as adults.**

- **Less aggressive behavior in childhood results in greater overall success in adulthood.**

- **Children with ADHD whose parents are emotionally healthy have less psychiatric and emotional problems.**

- **Children with ADHD who get along with their parents have fewer behavior problems and less aggressive behavior** than children who have a lot of conflict with their parents.

- **Less severe ADHD results in better academic achievement.**

SOURCE: Barkley, R.A. Attention Deficit Hyperactivity Disorder. New York: Guildford Press, 1990, p. 123-124.

Going Off to College

It is well known that students who get education beyond high school are likely to earn more money than those who do not. It is also known that students with ADHD are less apt to seek education beyond high school. ADHD does not affect one's intelligence, but it makes it more difficult to organize and complete the work that is required in school. The more we can help and prepare students with ADHD for some sort of specialized training after high school, the more successful they will be.

College is not for everyone. However, students can choose vocational training programs, two-year community college programs or four-year college or university programs.

Once your child leaves home, they may have the same problems but be without your support and assistance. The following guidelines, written for adolescents, can help your young adult think about his or her needs.

- **Learn and understand as much about ADHD as possible.** Know your strengths and how ADHD affects your performance and behavior.

- **Know what medications you are taking and why.** The more you know, the better. You may think taking medicine is a hassle. You may have heard yourself say, "I hate taking this stuff," or "I take medication because my parents make me." Remember, that when you are taking your medication, you are taking care of yourself. Your parents are not "making" you take it in attempts to control you.

  Learn as much about your medication as possible—what it is, when to take it, when not to take it. Do not share your medication with others. Do not take medication to stay up late and cram for test.

- **Practice time management.** You will not have parents to get you out of bed or off to work or school on time.

- **Practice pacing yourself.** Since attending class may not be required and grades are based on one or two tests, planning is essential. Putting off work until the last minute could spell disaster.

- **Learn study skills.** Learn what kind of environment you need to study successfully. You may need to find a quiet room or get ear phones to block out music or noise from roommates.

- **Be a list maker.** People with ADHD should be the "list makers of the world" since they often have weak short-term memories. Use a daily and weekly planner to keep track of assignments, tests and appointments. Help yourself remember.

- **Practice good health habits.** Nobody will be around to tell you what or when or when to sleep and exercise. However, regular habits in all of these areas will help you stay healthy, perform at your best and protect you from getting worn down.

- **Get help as often as you need it.** Your student advisor may be helpful in planning schedules and choosing living arrangements. Ask for help from instructors *before* you get behind, and get tutoring if you need it. It is better to get help early than to experience unnecessary frustration or failure.

- **Build a support system.** Get yourself a "coach" if possible to assist you with organizational skills, time management techniques, follow-through and overall support.

SOURCE: Kratz, L.J. Transitioning into college for the student with ADHD. The ADHD Challenge newsletter. 1998, p. 3-10.

ADHD in Adults

While a child is being assessed for ADHD, parents may realize they have many of the same symptoms (or did as a child). This is because ADHD is often an inherited condition.

ADHD in adults has now been studied for about 25 years. For a long time, researchers believed that children outgrew ADHD. Most experts now say that at least 50 percent of children with ADHD continue to have symptoms as adults. Paul Wender, MD, an expert in adults with ADHD, has described how the symptoms of ADHD seen in a child may look differently in adults.

- **Short attention span.** Adults continue to have trouble focusing their attention when required to do so. Problems with distractibility and weak short-term memory may also persist. Many adults with ADHD have learned to cope with their condition by working in jobs where they do not need to focus on one thing for long periods of time.

- **Hyperactivity.** Fidgeting and restlessness replace motoric hyperactivity. Adults with ADHD may be uncomfortable sitting still for long periods of time. They may dislike being inactive and have trouble relaxing.

- **Impulsivity.** This continues to be a major problem for adults with ADHD. They may have trouble keeping jobs and relationships because they often act before they think.

- **Disorganization.** Messy offices and households, an inability to keep track of belongings, and maintaining schedules can create major problems for adults.

- **Social interactions.** Having difficulty following directions and being described as "bossy" and controlling can make relationships difficult.

- **Emotional control.** Mood swings, boredom, low frustration tolerance and temper control are common with adults with ADHD.

- **Behavior problems.** Adults with ADHD who also have antisocial behaviors (such as conduct disorder) have more problems in all areas of their lives.

- **Medication response.** Medications work as well in adults as they do in children.

Adults who think they have symptoms of ADHD should seek help from their primary care provider. Medication, counseling and education about ADHD can be very helpful.

If you are like many parents of children with ADHD, you have probably felt completely alone at times—tired, confused, frustrated, and wondering where to turn next. **You're not alone.** There are many people, organizations, and resources that can help you cope with your child's ADHD. Here are a few suggestions:

Your Child's Primary Caregiver

If you have questions about having your child tested for ADHD, or about medication and follow-up, contact your family doctor or pediatrician first. Most doctors are well-prepared to assist you in this area. In addition, your insurance company may require that you see your primary caregiver before seeing a specialist.

Specialists

If your child has learning difficulties or serious behavior problems, seek the help of someone who specializes in these areas. In addition, public schools are mandated to provide services to students identified with special needs. Get help as early and as often as you need it–solving small problems now is much easier than solving major ones later!

Organizations

The following organizations offer classes and support services to caregivers and people with ADHD and/or learning disabilities. While this listing includes primarily Minnesota resources, there are similar organizations throughout the United States and Canada. Contact your health care provider for more information.

Chapter 7

Getting Additional Help

DOCTOR 555-7123
TEACHER 525-3971
MINISTER 321-8872
COUNSELOR 521-3111
FRIENDS 371-922
GRANDPARENTS 827-1970

National Organizations

■ **A.D.D. WareHouse**
300 Northwest 70th Avenue, Suite 102
Plantation, FL 33317
(800) 233-9273/FAX (954) 792-8545
http://www.addwarehouse.com

■ **CHADD**
(Children and Adults with Attention Deficit Disorder)
8181 Professional Place, Suite 201
Landover, MD 20785
(800) 233-4050/FAX (301) 306-7090
http://www.chadd.org

■ **NADDA**
(National Attention Deficit Disorder Association)
P.O. Box 1303
Northbrook, IL 60065
http://www.add.org

■ **American Academy of Child and Adolescent Psychiatry**
3615 Wisconsin Avenue NW
Washington, DC 20016-3007
(202) 966-7300/FAX (202) 966-2891
http://www.aacap.org

Local Organizations

■ **ADHD Parent Group**
Park Nicollet Clinic HealthSystem Minnesota
Alexander Center for Child Development and Behavior
5320 Hyland Greens Drive
Bloomington, MN 55437
(612) 993-2498

■ **Twin Cities CHADD Chapter**
c/o ARC of Hennepin County
Diamond Hills Center, Suite 140, 4301 Highway 7
Minneapolis, MN 55416
(612) 920-0855

■ **Learning Disabilities of Minnesota**
400 Selby Avenue, Suite D
St. Paul, MN 55102
(651) 222-0311 or (800) 488-4395/FAX (612) 222-0311

■ **PACER Center, Inc.**
(Parent Advocacy Coalition for Educational Rights)
4826 Chicago Avenue
Minneapolis, MN 55417-1055
(612) 827-2966, (800) 53-PACER (in Minnesota only)
http://www.pacer.org

ADHD Books for Parents and Teachers

Note: Most of the books listed in this chapter are available from the A.D.D. WareHouse, Inc., 300 Northwest 70th Avenue, Suite 102 Plantation, FL 33317. For catalog: Phone: (800) 233-9273; Fax: (954) 792-8545

Bain, L.J. A Parent's Guide to Attention Deficit Disorders. New York: Dell Publishing, 1991.

Barkley, R.A. Attention Deficit Hyperactivity Disorder: A Handbook for Diagnosis and Treatment. New York: The Guilford Press, 1990.

Garber, S.W.; Garber, M.D. and Spizman, R.F. If Your Child Is Hyperactive, Inattentive, Impulsive, Distractible. New York: Villard Books, 1990.

Ingersoll, B. Your Hyperactive Child. New York: Doubleday Press, 1988.

O'Leary, K.D. Mommy I Can't Sit Still. Liberty Corner, NJ: New Horizon Press Publishers, 1989.

Parker, H. The ADD Hyperactivity Workbook for Parents, Teachers, and Kids. Plantation, FL: Impact Publications, Inc., 1988.

Rief, S. How to Reach and Teach ADD and ADHD Children. Parmus, NJ: Center for Applied Research in Education, 1993.

Wender, P. The Hyperactive Child, Adolescent and Adult. Cambridge: Oxford University Press, 1987.

ADHD Books for Children and Teens

Amen, A.J. and Johnson, S. A Teenager's Guide to ADD. Fairfield, CA: Mindworks Press, 1996.

Gordon, M. I Would If I Could: A Teenager's Guide to ADHD/Hyperactivity. New York, NY: GSI Publications, 1993.

Gordon, M. My Brother's A World-Class Pain: A Sibling's Guide to ADHD/Hyperactivity. New York: GSI Publications, 1993.

Nadeau, K. Learning to Slow Down and Pay Attention. Annandale, VA: Chesapeake Psychological Publications, 1993.

Quinn, P. and Stern, J. Putting on the Brakes. Rockville, MD: Magination Press, 1991.

Books on Learning

Cummings, R. and Fisher, G. The School Survival Guide for Kids with LD. Minneapolis, MN: Free Spirit Publishing, 1993.

Cummings, R. and Fisher, G. The Survival Guide for Teenagers with LD. Minneapolis, MN: Free Spirit Publishing, 1990.

Johnson, S. Taking the Anxiety out of Test Taking. Oakland, CA: New Harbinger Publications, 1997.

Lauren, J. Succeeding with LD. Minneapolis, MN: Free Spirit Publishing, 1997.

Levine, M. Keeping a Head in School. Cambridge: Educators Publishing Service, 1992.

Levine, M. All Kinds of Minds. Cambridge: Educators Publishing Service, 1992.

Radencich, M.C. and Schumm, J.S. How to Help Your Child with Homework. Minneapolis, MN: Free Spirit Press, 1997.

Rief, Sandra. The ADD/ADHD Checklist. Parmus, NJ: Prentice Hall, 1997.

Silver, L. Dr. Larry Silver's Advice to Parents on Attention Deficit Hyperactivity Disorder. Washington, DC: American Psychiatric Press, 1993.

About the Author

Rebecca Kajander, BSN, RN, CPNP, MPH, is a pediatric nurse practitioner who has cared for children for 28 years. She has participated in the assessment and behavioral management of children with ADHD for 19 years.

She can be reached at the following address:

Rebecca Kajander
c/o Park Nicollet HealthSource
3800 Park Nicollet Boulevard
Minneapolis, MN 55417

Acknowledgements

Many people helped this book become a reality. My colleagues at the Alexander Center contributed many recommendations. Judy Alexander provided encouragement, support and assistance throughout the entire process. Suzanne Bennett, Kathy King and Linda Olson orchestrated production. Marsha Drew did an excellent job of expressing my ideas. The illustrations by J Campbell brought the content to life. My sincere thanks.

—*Becky Kajander*

This book was developed by the Institute for Research and Education HealthSystem Minnesota with funding support from The Alexander Memorial Fund, The Health Education Center of the Institute for Research and Education and employees, patients and friends of Park Nicollet HealthSystem Minnesota.

Author
Rebecca Kajander, CPNP, MPH

Editors
Marsha K. Drew
Jeanne Mettner

Contributors
Judy Alexander, MA
Suzanne Bennett, MPH
Kathy King , BS
Linda Olson, BS

Reviewers
ALEXANDER CENTER FOR
CHILD DEVELOPMENT AND
BEHAVIOR
Medical Staff
Timothy P. Culbert, MD
Rebecca Kajander, CPNP, MPH
Barbara J. Kratz, CPNP, MSN
Judson B. Reaney, MD
Psychologists
Stephen Bonfilio, PhD, Director
Lynda Richtsmeier, Cyr, PhD
Jan Goodsitt, PhD
Carmen Gutterman, PhD
Stephen Olson, PhD
Speech Language Pathologists
Kathleen Bykowski, MS CCC
Michele Dorenkamp, MS CCC
Educational Consultant
Johanna Westby, MS, SpEd

EDUCATION
Colleen Faber
Martha E. Fahden
Martha S. Reed, M Ed
Nancy Moore Smith
Barbara Sorum
Patricia Steingruebl, MA

MEDICAL/HEALTH CARE
Michael Blum, PhD
Anne R. Gearity, MSW
Morris Green, MD
Terril H. Hart, MD
Kathleen Sweetman, MD

PARENT
Ruth Dolan
Ann Goodmundson
Ruth Gregory
Susan Hanson
David Kihm
Lydia Kihm
Theresa Palmersheim

Designer
ArtVille, Inc.

Illustrator
J Campbell

The information in this book does not necessarily reflect the opinions and recommendations of each individual contributor, reviewer or supporter. The book cannot serve as a substitute for a physician's medical care. and cannot be used to diagnose medical conditions or prescribe treatment.